STAFFORD CLIFF

1000 GARDEN IDEAS

Quadrille

Plants aren't the only thing that you need to think about when you are creating a garden. In fact – with so many gardening programmes, magazine articles and books around – plants are now one of the easiest things to find, especially when there are so many plant suppliers and nurseries around the world. But what about all the other decisions you need to make? The paths, the paving, the pots, the fencing and the gate? Would you like a bench and a table, a water feature, a birdhouse or a bridge? What should they look like? How will they fit into the rest of your garden scheme? And how can you make them look more individual, more creative or more effective? Whatever you want to do, someone has done it before, and if you've ever been to visit other gardens, country houses or local garden open-days, you will have realised that this is the best way to pick up good ideas – if only you could store them away until you need them; if only you could find so many that you'd have lots of choices for every gardening problem you're ever likely to need to solve; if only you could gather them all into an album of garden ideas. Now you don't need to. For the first time, they're all here – forty years of visiting gardens with a designer's eye, to spot the cleverest solutions, the best answers, the most original choices, and present them all in the most comprehensive collection of garden ideas you could ever find.

GATES

Walk up and down your street, explore your neighbourhood, your town. Why are all the front gates so boring? A front gate is an opportunity to show how individual we are, how creative, how inventive. Perhaps, because they tend to be made from either wood or metal, they perish or rust away more quickly than other garden elements like walls and paths. If your gate is at the back of the house, or in a side wall, it will be a different size and shape to one at the front. Sometimes, when we move in, they're missing altogether, and we're at a loss to know what design to choose or, indeed, if we need one at all. On the other hand, in a street where all the houses are built in the same style or the same period, maybe there is a perception that the gate belongs more to the façade of the building than to the planting or the personality of the owner. Certainly there are streets in London or Paris or Sydney or Charleston, where all the fences and gates are part of the urban architecture and you cannot change even the colour. For the rest, look around for something that suits you, your home and the way you live. Think of it as a chance to add a little design flourish that would be inappropriate on a larger scale – like a stamp on a letter.

WALLS &
FENCES

The frame to your horticultural composition is the fence or wall. Start by answering three simple questions: do you want to see it or cover it up with some sort of climbing plant? Do you want to see through it or block out what is beyond? Finally, do you want to keep something out or keep something in? For various reasons, most of us need a fence, but not one so high that it blocks out the light and causes conflict with our neighbours. If you only need to define the margins of your domain, then a simple post and rail job will do. But, for most gardeners, it's one of the defining factors that finishes off the space, provides an element of protection and a vertical surface with which to be creative. And creativity is the key, because there is now an unlimited supply of possibilities, from mellow old brick, drystone or cracked pebbles, to concrete, ribbed and perforated metal, corrugated iron or glass bricks. Some are permanent; some more temporary. Some harmonise with the style of the house; others create a contrast. Some let light through; some retain the heat and block the wind. Some you can assemble yourself, buying the components and taking them home in the car; some might require a carpenter, a bricklayer or a builder; for some you might need a reclamation yard or even an antique dealer.

TILES, PATHS &
PAVING

When it comes to the surface underfoot, there are a number of elements to consider, but of course it depends on the area you intend to cover. If it's a narrow front path then it will be one of the first things people see when they arrive; if it's a large area at the back of the house or in the heart of the garden, then it will contribute as much to your scheme as the planting, particularly if you look down on it from the upstairs windows. The graphic quality of what you decide to do is important both from up close as you stand on it, and from afar. But how does it 'feel' to walk on – smooth and firm, spongy and organic, or rough and uneven – or is it a combination? It could be smooth where you're meant to walk and rough where you're not. It could progress gradually from one material to another, one colour to another, or one scale to another. Do you want it to look rustic, like a path in harmony with nature, or modern and 'architectural', part of the built environment? How will it change when it's wet or even icy? When it's covered with leaves or blossom or moss? Will it turn out to be an ongoing nightmare to maintain, or will it improve with age? Lastly, think about how it sounds. Gravel will alert you to approaching visitors, but woodchip, pebbles, slate shards and glass beads all produce a variety of interesting sounds, and say a lot more about you and your flair as a creative gardener.

EDGING

If a garden is a poem or a short story, then edging is the punctuation and a fence is a full stop. Edgings are vital to the flow of the planting, joining one phrase to another, coordinating a number of different or similar ideas and knitting the picture together. Yet, if they are so important, why are they so often overlooked or uninspired? Look at the horizontal surfaces in a garden as a number of personalities meeting each other. Some, like flowers and low hedges, get on well together, whereas others – hard and soft characters, like lawn and path – are best kept apart. How the edging works will depend on the style of your garden; if it's rustic or cottagey your solution will be found in the countryside – rocks, little fences or, perhaps, an old log; if it's contemporary your answers are more likely to come from urban architecture and the use of modern materials – concrete, steel, slate, brick, acrylic or even glass. Finally, if you're feeling creative, consider recycling something. Blue bottles sunk upside down into the earth, broken frost-free terracotta pots, or even old dinner plates, half-embedded. Failing all else, there are the products that are made for the job: moulded tiles, glazed terracotta rope segments, latticed willow hurdles or reproduction-antique French iron railings.

STEPS

More than perhaps any other element in the garden, I think steps are the most fascinating, with the most possibilities. They take us from one level to another, they change our perspective of the space, and they present endless opportunities for creativity. From the bottom we see one aspect – the risers or upright bits; from the top we see the treads; in mid-flight we see both. So, why are they so often dull and ignored, grey concrete or drab stone? Perhaps we are afraid to do anything too creative in case it looks confusing and unsafe? Perhaps – if we have inherited them – they are too difficult to replace. Perhaps we just need inspiration. Adding different levels to a garden can be a costly and daunting prospect and, consequently, steps are usually limited to only two or three wide treads. On the other hand, many of the most fascinating gardens are hilly, with steps that wind up out of sight, turn a corner, or stop and start seemingly at will. Steps also afford all sorts of areas for planting, they need a beginning and an end, and they need edges – all providing a chance to embellish. At the same time, many homes are built on hills, or have steps – often half a dozen or so – up to the entrance. Why should they be any less important a chance for self-expression than the gate, the path or, indeed, the front door?

POTS

Pots are, perhaps, the most flexible of all the elements in the garden. You can move them around until you find the best position, you can bring them forward when the plants they contain are in flower, and you can, of course, change the plants as often as you like. You can, and I hope you will, have lots of pots in lots of shapes and sizes, like hats to top off different outfits, or bright colourful ties to dress up the same dark suit. But pots are not just for plants, they can contain water, pebbles, twigs or even fish. They are available in an abundance of different materials with a plain or matte finish, glazed in rich colours, or embellished with a multitude of designs. More elaborate containers look best with modest sculptural contents, whereas a showy cascading plant might need a simpler pot. Finally, there are the urns, the Dowager Duchesses of the pot, which have a design heritage that can be traced back to the Renaissance. Aloof on a plinth, they are an object in their own right. Though pots are currently the most fashionable design accessory in the garden don't be limited by what you see in the shops. Search out reclamation yards, specialist potteries, or even find a local potter and commission him or her to create your own shape, or copy one of the examples that follow.

CHAIRS, SEATS &
BENCHES

A bench is not only a place to sit. Whether it's made from wood or concrete, stone or metal, a bench (or a seat) also functions like a piece of sculpture – an object that adds to the composition of your garden and a relief from the soft planting. The size, the form and the design of the piece – and where you place it – are as important as what it's like to sit on. It should be comfortable, but it should also look comfortable – as well as being in keeping with the size and style of your garden: classical and grand, modern and architectural, or twiggy and rustic. Some benches are meant to stay out all year round, growing more attractive as they slowly weather, acquiring a patina of moss or rust. Others are too fragile and are designed to fold away after the summer. Some of the best have tailor-made or improvised cushions that appear each morning, and some – perhaps close to the house – form part of a cluster of furniture that provides a spot for lunches or candlelit summer suppers. But, on its own, a bench is also a marker. It says that over here there is a nice viewpoint, the best vista, the most sheltered/sunny aspect or a shady, cool retreat. It signals to everyone that, if you sit for a while, you won't be disappointed.

STATUES
& OTHER OBJECTS

The tradition of having statues dotted around your garden goes back to the Italian gardens of the 16th century and beyond. They were thought to compel interest, stimulate imagination, strengthen memory and discourage trivial and selfish thoughts. The statue – particularly of the human body – had the effect of commanding your attention and perhaps, if it was a good copy of a classical work, your admiration. Nowadays, really wonderful pieces of garden statuary have become highly sought after and tend to fetch colossal prices – even those that are badly weathered and with bits missing. In fact, the more weathered the better. But such pieces can also be difficult to integrate well into a modest town garden, and mass-produced, scaled-down copies are considered as kitsch as gnomes and fairies. Consider, instead, other objects that will also give focus, create shape or add a bit of tension: old chimney pots, architectural fragments, sundials, columns, urns, obelisks – even a fallen branch or an attractively shaped rock. Alternatively, there are plenty of sculptors, potters or metalworkers making things that you might find suitable. Finally, don't forget the smaller things: think about wind chimes, mobiles and, most environmentally friendly of all, houses for birds, bats, hedgehogs and even ladybirds.

ROCKS

Rocks and stones in a garden represent millions of years of accumulated time. The Japanese used rocks as far back as the 7th century A.D. and some believed they symbolised the unchanging female, whereas plants were male. In both Japan and China, their gardens developed the art of the naturalistic landscape, with rivers, lakes and bridges. Later on, small urban courtyards used one or two large, beautifully shaped rocks to symbolise a distant mountain, and consequently they became highly prized both financially and artistically. More recently, rocks were also incorporated into aristocratic English gardens, as landscape gardeners built hillsides, waterfalls and grottos, in which a hermit was supposed to live. Today, rocks are still as important to gardens, are just as expensive and hold the same mythical qualities. It's about yin and yang. Hard and soft landscaping has been developed by garden designers to be as appropriate to a tiny town garden or a roof terrace as it is to a huge country estate. Rocks, from water-washed pebbles to jagged rocks and giant boulders, are readily available — some even pre-drilled to use as water features. But, unlike most other garden elements, it's harder to imagine the effect, plan the results, and avoid mistakes with an item that may take four men to lift.

WATER

POOLS, FOUNTAINS & BRIDGES

Every garden needs water. The plants need it to grow, birds and insects need it, and you need it, too. Water has been an intrinsic part of garden design since the Ancient Egyptians four thousand years ago. The Persians thought that no land beyond the sight of water could be considered a garden; their walled enclosures included streams and fountains that cooled the air and created what they called paradise. In Italy, during the Renaissance – utilising the hilly locations of many of the palaces – some of the most imaginative garden schemes were based on water being pumped to the top of the hill and allowing it to flow down again, passing through a multitude of ingenious spouts, jets and runnels. Grand country houses also had gardens that included natural looking ponds, lakes, rivers and streams. In your own garden the choices are more straightforward. If you don't have a spring, a well or a local river to divert, try creating your own natural looking pond, stream, canal, rill or cascade using the various techniques that are available to you today. Water can be still, its reflective surface adding extra light to your garden; it can bubble over rocks, trickle from a spout, or spray in a multitude of fountain effects. With water you will add, perhaps, the most relaxing, most magical quality of all: sound.

PERGOLAS, GAZEBOS & FOLLIES

Every country has its tradition of small garden structures. In Scandinavia, they are often intended for spending the day by the sea; in Japan, they are teahouses; in Indian palaces they were sometimes used to accommodate musicians, who would add their music to the other garden delights. In grand English gardens, miniature cottages, cabins and summerhouses were places for children to play, or adults to take tea – and there was always the possibility of the occasional illicit liaison. Some of these houses even had a fireplace and running water. At the opposite extreme were the belvederes, temples, follies and mock ruins that were often sited on distant hilltops in order to add visual interest and hint at Arcadian frivolity. More practical are the garden structures which, whilst sometimes framing a view, are primarily to support vines, roses and other climbing plants. These are the arches, the pergolas and the arbours, where the experience of walking beneath or through them, or sitting under them, is as important as their effect from afar. Whilst a long pergola is suitable only for larger spaces, or to transform an awkward area along one side of a town house garden, an arch is ideal for creating a focal point, embracing a seat or showcasing a spectacular flowering climber.

PARTERRES, HEDGES &
TOPIARY

The art of pruning and trimming trees and bushes goes back to before the Romans, who practised it to excess. It was revived again in the Middle Ages and was a craze in the 17th, and again in the 19th, centuries. Hedges – whether privet, yew, box, holly, holm oak, horn beam or cypress – make an effective windbreak, a good background to plants and a way of dividing a large garden into a variety of interesting and theatrical spaces. Really big hedges can take two or three hundred years to achieve, and ingenious ladder structures to maintain. In Japan, cutting and controlling the shape of trees and shrubs is an intrinsic part of gardening, even in city squares and at traffic roundabouts. In Bangkok, and other parts of Thailand, topiary and its cousin bonsai adorn every temple and shrine. In France they developed the art of the parterre and in England we have our own take on the art, as peacocks and small dogs in village cottage gardens contrast with massive compositions of imagination and caprice on grand estates. At its most modest level, you might start with a specimen tree in the centre of the lawn, or two rosemary bushes beside the front door. Whatever you choose, they will all require the same love of living sculpture, and the same passion for pruning.

VISTAS

A vista provides a journey for the eye. It may not tell you the whole story but, like a trailer in the cinema or on TV, it gives you a view into something further away – through a gap in the hedge, under an arch of climbing roses, down a narrow pathway or through a door in a wall. The very first gardens, thousands of years ago, were walled enclosures. In the early 15th century, as Italian merchants began to build their villas outside the heat of the cities, they discovered that an opening in the wall of their garden gave them an attractive view of the countryside. Soon, the walled enclosure was removed altogether, and the view – or partial view – was the thing. Depending on where you live, the view can reveal a tower on a hilltop miles away or a pot on a stand, a piece of sculpture or a tree across the road. Vistas are about hiding and revealing, sometimes obscuring a view in order to tempt you with only a glimpse of it at first. They are the amuse bouche of gardening, the tasty morsel of which there may not be any more. Because, at its least, a vista may only be a promise of something which is not yours and which you cannot get to. But, by framing it and focussing on it, you are saying 'this is also part of my garden, and my garden, by definition, is part of the wider world'.

COLOUR

Plants are, of course, the most exciting part of gardening – the only point, some might say. Planning a garden, putting in your plants or bulbs or cuttings – and watching them grow – goes to the heart of gardening, and there can be nothing more therapeutic, more gratifying or more primal. Millions of people around the world get tremendous pleasure from visiting gardens and garden centres, looking at flowers and acquiring new varieties. In the late 19th century, the status of an English aristocrat was based, among other things, on the number of bedding plants his gardeners planted – sometimes as many as 50,000. But there is another aspect of gardening that is much more difficult to get right, and that is composition. It is the skill of a great chef to decide what goes with what to produce the most interesting flavours and bring out the best of all the ingredients. So it is with gardening, and it's not only about colour and soil and sun. Buy everything you like, stick it all in, and you'll get a hotchpotch of riotous joy. But, be more selective, restrict your colour palette, think about the size and scale of plants, the foliage colour and leaf shapes, and you will be rewarded with a much more subtle effect. Think of it as the difference between a brass band concert and a violin concerto.

USEFUL ADDRESSES

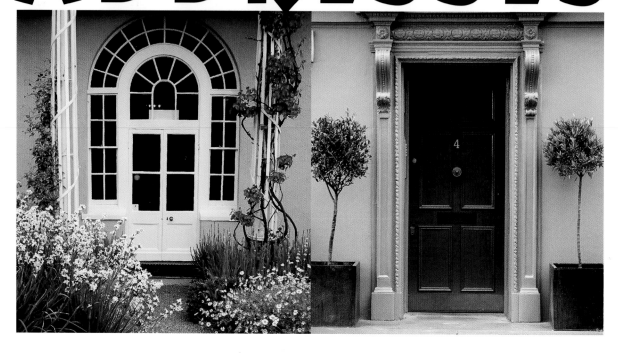

Adirondack Outdoors
24 Southern Way, Farnborough
Hampshire GU14 0RE
01252 642513
www.adirondack.co.uk

Manufacturer of high quality outdoor furniture, primarily in the Adirondack style, built using naturally durable materials and with emphasis on comfort and style.
Page 99, row 3, no. 1

African Thatch Company Ltd
Unit 2, Low Mill Workshops
Phoenix Business Centre
Low Mill Road, Ripon
North Yorkshire HG4 1NS
0845 3700 445
www.africanthatchcompany.co.uk

African-style gazebos made from wooden poles and South African cape reed thatch tiles.

Agriframes
Journal House, Hartcliffe Way
Bristol BS3 5RJ
0845 260 4450
www.agriframes.co.uk

Metal arches, obelisks, gazebos, pergolas and screens.

Apta
Dencora Way, Leacon Road
Fairwood Business Park
Ashford, Kent TN23 4FH
01233 621090
www.apta.co.uk

Supplies a comprehensive range of pots to garden centres, ranging from metal, terracotta to various ceramic finishes.

Barlow Tyrie Ltd
Braintree
Essex CM7 2RN
01376 557600
www.teak.com

Seats, benches and garden furniture in teak.

Bellamont Topiary
Long Bredy, Dorset DT2 9HN
01308 482220
www.bellamont-topiary.co.uk

Largest collection of field-grown box topiary and hedging in the UK. Plants sold by shape (sphere, cone, cube, spiral, egg, onion, pyramid, fondant) and size.

Benchmark Furniture
Bath Road, Kintbury
Hungerford, Berkshire RG17 9SA
01488 608020
www.benchmark-furniture.com

Excellence in design, materials and craftsmanship, producing contemporary classics that will last a lifetime. Designed by well-known names including the Azumis, Terence Conran, Thomas Heatherwick and Russell Pinch.
Page 86, bottom left
Page 97, bottom left

Bradstone
Aggregate Industries UK Ltd
Holland Ward, Ashbourne
Derbyshire DE6 3ET
0800 975 9828
www.bradstone.com

Paving, 'log' sleepers, decorative aggregates (cobbles, stones, rocks), edging and walling.

Augustus Brandt Antiques
Media House, Pound Street
Petworth, West Sussex GU28 0DX
01798 344722
www.augustus-brandt-antiques.co.uk

Antique garden furniture and pots.

The Brooke Pottery
Low Crossett, Chop Gate
Bilsdale, Middlesbrough TS9 7LH
01434 748032
www.thebrookepottery.com

Collection of large English urns, classically designed with a strong contemporary edge. All urns are handmade from high-firing English terracotta clay using the traditional skills of hand-throwing, coiling and press moulding.

Bulbeck Foundry
Unit 9, Reach Road, Burwell
Cambridgeshire CB5 0AH
01638 743153 | 0870 780 4895
www.bulbeckfoundry.co.uk

English lead statuary, urns, cisterns and pots.

Bygones Architectural Reclamation (Canterbury) Ltd
Nackington Road, Canterbury
Kent CT4 7BA
0800 0433012 | 01227 767453

Water features, statuary, gates, bricks, tiles, railway sleepers, paving, rocks, edging.

Cannock Gates
Martindale, Hawks Green
Cannock, Staffordshire
WS11 7XT
0870 754 7575
www.cannockgates.co.uk

Large selection of gates.

Capital Garden Products Ltd
Gibbs Reed Barn
Pashley Road, Ticehurst
East Sussex TN5 7HE
01580 201092
www.capital-garden.com

Decorative plant containers and architectural features. Also bespoke solutions tailored to clients' needs. Worldwide delivery.
Opposite page 1
Page 63, row 3, no.1
Page 71, row 4, no.2
Page 75, row 2, no. 1
Page 97, row 3, no.1

Chairworks Ltd
47 Weir Road
London SW19 8UG
0208 247 3700
www.chairworks.info

Plant climbers, covers, arbours, gazebos, benches, edgings and fence panels (hurdles) made of hazel or willow.
Page 31, row 3, no.2
Page 88, bottom left

Chameleon Aquifers
Holloway Farm, Milton Common
Thame, Oxfordshire OX9 2JX
0800 0933 656 | 01844 278333

Products to create water features, from Monolith Aquifers with their impressive size and rugged natural beauty, through to Granite and Marble Aquifer ranges.

Chilstone
Victoria Park, Fordcombe Road
Langton Green, Kent TN3 0RE
01892 740866
www.chilstone.com

Traditional garden ornaments, pots, urns, troughs, plinths, fountains, birdbaths, statues, dovecotes and sculpture.
Page 71, row 2, no.3
Page 114, centre bottom

John Close Sundials
10 Centaur Way, Maldon
Essex CM9 6XU
01621 851994
www.johnclosesundials.co.uk

Large range of quality made sundials, armillary sundials, wall dials and horizontal dials.

Connoisseur Sundials
Lane's End, Strefford
Craven Arms
Shropshire SY7 8DE
01588 672126
www.sun-dials.net

Accurate sundials and armillary spheres. Handmade in brass and bronze.

Coulson's Bridges
Broome Hill, Marten's Lane
Polstead CO6 5AQ
01206 262387
www.coulsonsbridges.co.uk

Elegant curved bridges individually crafted to any design.

Andrew Crace
Bourne Lane, Much Hadham
Hertfordshire SG10 6ER
01279 842685
www.andrewcrace.co.uk

Garden seats, benches, tables, sun-loungers, tree-seats and planters. Handmade in iroko or oak.
Page 82, row 1, no.2
Page 82, row 2, no.1 & 2
Page 82, row 3, no.1 & 2
Page 83, top left
Page 84, row 2, no.2 & 3
Page 84, row 3, no.2
Page 85, row 4, no.2
Page 86, row 1, no.1 & 2
Page 86, row 2, no.1
Page 86, row 3, no.1 & 2
Page 94, bottom right

Cranborne Stone
West Orchard, Shaftesbury
Dorset SP7 0LJ
01258 472685
www.cranbornestone.co.uk

Balustrading, finials, coping stones, urns, planters in hand-cast, reconstituted stone. Standard and bespoke designs.

Creta Cotta
Jubilee Cottage, Penrhos
Raglan, Monmouthshire NP15 2LF
01600 780416
www.cretacotta.co.uk

Handmade frost-proof cretan terracotta pots.

The Cutting Edge Collection
The Secret Courtyard
Hillier Garden Centre
London Road, Windlesham
Surrey GU20 6LQ
01252 835735
www.cutting-edge.gb.com

Arbours, gazebos and summerhouses. Also a few bronze, resin bronze or lead water features and ornaments.

Cyan
Unit 6, Coulsdon North
Industrial Estate
Station Approach, Coulsdon
Surrey CR5 2NR
0845 6789 340
www.cyan-teak-furniture.com

Benches, garden furniture, tubs and plants.

Design and Landscape
Bawdon lodge, Nanpantan,
Loughborough
Leicestershire LE12 9XJ
01509 261700
www.designandlandscape.co.uk

Contemporary sculpture, water features, furniture, pots and planters.

Dorset Reclamation
Cow Drove, Bere Regis
Wareham, Dorset BH20 7JZ
01929 472200
www.dorsetreclamation.co.uk

Decorative architectural and garden antiques, including flagstones, paving bricks, quarry tiles, stone troughs, birdbaths, benches, statues, staddle stones, urns & gates.

Gary Drostle
40 Strand House, Merbury Close,
London SE28 0LU
0208 316 7734
www.drostle.com
www.mosaicmakers.co.uk

Mosaic artist with a useful website on how to commission a mosaic.

Eden Furniture Ltd
36 Wood Road, Codsall
South Staffordshire WV8 1DB
01902 847955
www.teak-furniture.co.uk

Garden furniture, benches and sun-loungers.

English Garden Carpentry Co. Ltd
The Old Milking Parlour
Brewer's Lane, West Tisted
Hampshire SO24 0HQ
01462 828000
www.egcc.biz

Arbours, bridges, gazebos, pavilions, pergolas, fencing, gates and bespoke garden structures.

English Hurdle
Curload Stoke St. Gregory
Taunton, Somerset TA3 6JD
01823 648418
www.hurdle.co.uk

Hurdles but also gates, arches, arbours using willow and similar materials.

Field Farm Enterprises Ltd
Field Farm, Field Lane
Solihull, West Midlands B91 2RT
0121 705 0833
www.cedarshed.co.uk

Lots of different sizes and shapes of gazebos in solid cedar.

Forest
Unit 291 & 296, Hartlebury
Trading Estate, Hartlebury
Worcestershire DY10 4JB
0870 191 9801
www.forestgarden.co.uk

The UK's largest manufacturer of wooden fences, arches, arbours, pergolas, trellis and planters.

Useful Addresses

Robert Foster
Unit C18 Maw's Craft Centre
Jackfield, Nr Ironbridge
Telford TF8 7LS
01746 861330
www.
sundialsbyrobertfoster.co.uk

Handmade sundials and
armillary spheres.

French Stone (UK) Ltd
Robins Cob, Fanshawe Lane
Henbury, Cheshire SK11 9PP
01260 224516
www.frenchstone.co.uk

French stone fountains,
benches, urns, statues and
ornaments made from cast
stone, sculpted stone or
terracotta.

Garden Iron
Four Oaks, Newent
Gloucestershire GL18 1LU
01531 890123
www.gardeniron.co.uk

Wrought-iron garden
structures, folding furniture
and plant supports.

Gardening Thoughts Ltd
Mushroom Farm, Mile Road
Reymerston, Norfolk NR9 4QZ
01362 822434
www.gardeningthoughts.co.uk

Tree seats, arbours, arches,
bridges, summerhouses and
log cabins.

Garpa
Garden and Park Furniture Ltd
Gibbs Reed Barn, Pashley Road
Ticehurst, East Sussex TN5 7HE
01580 201190
www.garpa.co.uk

Over 25 years' experience and
a passion for the garden have
led to the development of
furniture and accessories for
discerning taste – timeless,
elegant and weatherproof.

Gaze Burville Ltd
Redloh House, 2 Michael Road
London SW6 2AD
0207 471 8500
www.gazeburville.com

Creating the finest English
outdoor furniture through an
honest commitment to design
integrity, comfort and
craftsmanship.
Page 82, row 4, no.2
Page 85, row 5, no.2

Global Gardens Ltd
Suite 127 Peel House
30 The Downs, Altrincham
Cheshire WA14 2PX
0800 970 4777
www.global-gardens.co.uk

Fine handmade Italian frost-
resistant pots, planters and
urns.

Gloster Furniture Ltd
Collins Drive, Severn Beach
Bristol BS35 4GG
01454 631450
www.gloster.com

From traditional to
contemporary, products to suit
all requirements and locations.
Benches, armchairs, tables,
chairs, sun-loungers and
occasional furniture.
Page 82, top left
Page 99, bottom left

Grange Fencing Ltd
Halesfield 21, Telford
Shropshire TF7 4PA
01452 682797
www.grangefen.co.uk

Arbours, gazebos, arches,
pergolas, gates and fencing.
Page 31, row 5, no.1, 2 & 3
Page 31, row 3, no.3
Page 99, bottom left

H. Crowther Ltd
5 High Road, Chiswick
London W4 2ND
0208 994 2326
www.hcrowther.co.uk

Large selection of antique
garden ornaments.

Haddonstone Ltd
The Forge House, East Haddon
Northampton NN6 8DB
01604 770711
www.haddonstone.com

Pots, urns, troughs, plinths,
pool and fountain accessories,
statuary, birdbaths, sundials,
garden furniture, balls and
lawn edgings.

David Harber Ltd
Valley Farm, Bix, Henley on
Thames, Oxon RG9 6BW
01491 576956
www.davidharber.com

Water features, sculptures and
sundials. Plinths in a range of
styles.

Christopher Hartnoll
Little Bray House, Brayford
North Devon EX32 7QG
01598 710245
www.christopherhartnoll.co.uk

Iron garden furniture.
Page 41, row 3, no.1

Heal's
196 Tottenham Court Road
London W1T 7LQ
08700 240780
www.heals.co.uk
for branches

Seasonal collections of stylish
outdoor furniture and
accessories.

Hillhout Ltd
Unit 18, Ellough Industrial Est
Beccles, Suffolk NR34 7TD
01502 718091
www.hillhout.nl

Manufacturer of sturdy
wooden garden products,
such as fencing, pergolas,
edgings, furniture, planters
and gazebos.

Hopes Grove Nurseries
Smallhyth Road, Tenderden
Kent TN30 7LT
01580 765600
www.hopesgrovenurseries.co.uk

Extensive lists of all types of
hedging plants and box and
yew topiary.

IOTA Garden and Home Ltd
Wick Road, Wick St Lawrence
North Somerset BS22 7YQ
01934 522617
www.iotagarden.com

Contemporary planters
(granite, fibreglass, slate and
terrazzo). Granite water
features and mirror polished
steel art.

The Iron Made Company
PO Box 1042, Lincoln LN5 5AF
0845 644 7072
www.ironmade.co.uk

Specialise in folding and easy
to assemble ironware
furniture for the home and
garden.

Italian Terrace
Pykards Hall, Rede
Bury St. Edmunds
Suffolk IP29 4AY
01284 789666
www.italianterrace.co.uk

A collection of urns, vases
and plaques handmade by
craftsmen in Italy.
Each piece, either classical
or contemporary, has a
wonderful aged and
weathered texture.

Jacksons
Stowting Common, Ashford
Kent TN25 6BN
0800 414343
www.jacksons-fencing.co.uk

Timber fencing, balustrades,
gates, trellis, pergolas and
planters. Also farm gates,
post and rail fencing, chain
mesh, cleft chestnut and
centry bar fencing.

Jade Pavilions
Unit 6 Underwood Business Park,
Wookey Hole Road
Wells, Somerset BA5 1AF
07967 640761
www.jade-pavilions.com

Tea-houses, temples, pavilions,
bridges and entrances.
Standard or custom designs.

JapanGarden.co.uk
15 Bank Crescent, Ledbury
Herefordshire HR8 1AA
01531 630091
www.japangarden.co.uk

Internet-based business
supplying all types of items
for Japanese gardens:
bamboo screens, water
features including deer
scarers, rocks, gazebos,
bridges etc

Juro Antiques
Whitbourne
Nr Worcester WR6 5SF
01886 821261
www.juro.co.uk

Wide assortment of garden
antiques, including stone
troughs, cidermills, staddle
stones, statuary, fountains
and garden furniture.

Kent Balusters
1 Gravesend Road, Strood
Rochester, Kent ME2 3PH
01634 711617
www.kentbalusters.co.uk

Balustrades, columns,
pergolas, temples, ball finials,
steps and paving.

**The Landscape Ornament
Company Ltd**
Long Barn, Patney
Devizes, Wiltshire SN10 3RB
01380 840533
www.landscapeornament.com

Timeless designs from
landscape architect Michael
Balston and contemporary
artists and sculptors. An
inspired range of timber
furniture, stone ornaments
and earthenware pots.
Page 84, row 3, no.1
Page 84, row 4, no.2
Page 84, row 5, no.1 & 2
Page 97, row 2, no.1

Chris Lewis
South Heighton Pottery
Nr Newhaven
East Sussex BN9 0HL
01273 514330
www.studiopottery.co.uk

Large and small garden pots,
garden seats and sculptural
pieces – all 100% frost-proof.
Also individual pieces and
special commissions.
Page 64, centre bottom
Page 96, row 2, no.2
Page 142, row 4, no.3

Magma Designs
Unit 12 Battersea Business
Centre, 99-109 Lavender Hill
London SW11 5QL
0207 2288 466

Wide range of pots, urns,
troughs and 'riverstone'
cobbled stone patterns
mounted on mesh – for floor
or wall covering.
Endpapers & Page 39 top right

Marshalls
Birkby Grange
Birkby Hall Road
Birkby, Huddersfield HD2 2YA
0870 120 7474
www.marshalls.co.uk

Paths, edging, walls,
decorative aggregates
(pebbles, cobbles, rocks,
glass).

Marston and Langinger Ltd
142 Ebury Street
London SW1 8UP
0207 881 5717
www.marston-and-
langinger.com

Selection of furniture in wire
for garden and conservatory.

Metallicus Ltd
Slade Lane, Rastrick
Brighouse HD6 3PP
01484 716651
www.metallicus.co.uk

Designs and builds
contemporary metal work
including: furniture, tree
seats, water features and
planters.

Chris Nangle Furniture Design
Unit 15, Site A Redual Industrial
Estate, West Felton
Shropshire SY11 4HS
01691 611864
www.chrisnanglefurniture.co.uk

Landscape furniture designed
and made from prime grade
UK oak and marine stainless
steel. All timber is from well-
managed woodlands in the UK.
Page 89, row 2, no.1
Page 102, row 3, no.2

Natural Driftwood Sculptures
Sunburst House, Elliott Road
Bournemouth BH11 8LT
01202 578274
www.driftwoodsculptures.co.uk

Originating from the lakes
of Canada, the Western Red
Cedar driftwood sculptures
have a unique silver colouring,
which complements their
wonderful shapes. Mail order.

New Dawn Furniture
Rose Cottage, Commonside
Westbourne, Emsworth
Hampshire PO10 8TD
01243 375535
www.newdawnfurniture.co.uk

Bespoke garden furniture in
oak or teak.

206

Useful Addresses

norton Garden Structures
The Studio, Upper norton
West Sussex PO20 9EA
01243 607690
www.
nortongardenstructures.co.uk

Gazebos, summerhouses, arbours, bridges, pergolas and garden art.

Oak Tree Pottery
Staddlestones, Yeovil Road
Halstock, Dorset BA22 9RR
01435 891486
www.oaktreepottery.co.uk

Original ceramic garden sculptures made to order in the studio.

Oakleaf Gates
The Old Hop Kilns
Westhide Court, Westhide
Hereford HR1 3RQ
01432 850100
www.oakleafgates.co.uk

Design and produce bespoke gates to the very highest standards of craftsmanship. All are constructed using seasoned oak.

Original Features
155 Tottenham Lane, Crouch End
London n8 9BT
0208 348 5155
www.originalfeatures.co.uk

Supplies products for restoring Olde English tiles such as black and white tiled paths.

Outer Eden Trading
Rear 43-45 Francis Street
Stoneygate, Leicester LE2 2BE
0116 270 8100
www.outer-eden.co.uk

Outdoor furniture with an emphasis on build, quality and style.

Oxford Planters Ltd
The Vine House, Heath Farm
Swerford, Chipping norton
Oxon OX7 4Bn
01608 683100
www.oxfordplanters.co.uk

Topiary (mostly box, yew and bay) in various shapes, plus a good range of containers (wooden from Belgium, galvanised metal from Paris and lead planters from Oxford.)

Oxley's Furniture Co Ltd
Lapstone Farm, Westington Hill
Chipping Campden
Gloucestershire GL55 6UR
01386 840466
www.oxleys.com

Handmade fine quality cast aluminium furniture, which is rust-proof, rot-proof and will completely withstand the effects of sun, wind and rain.

Plantstuff Ltd
The Anglo Trading Estate
Shepton Mallet
Somerset BA4 5BY
0870 774 3366
www.plantstuff.com

Small birdhouses, feeders and nesting boxes. Butterfly, ladybird and hedgehog houses. Mail order.

Pots and Pithoi
The Barns, East Street
Turner's Hill
West Sussex RH10 4QQ
01342 714793
www.potsandpithoi.com

Painted teak garden furniture, plus claims to have the world's largest selection of Cretan terracotta pots.

Quercus UK Ltd
The Laurels
Queen Street
Keinton Mandeville
Somerset TA11 6EG
01458 223378
sales@quercusfencing.co.uk

Stylish oak fencing panels that allow air to pass through.

Railway Sleeper.com
Owthorpe Road, Cotgrave
nottingham nG12 3PU
0115 9890445
www.railwaysleeper.com

Can supply and deliver 20 types of railway sleeper, a website lists hundreds of examples of sleeper projects.

Room In The Garden
no1 River Ground Stables
The Walled Garden
The Ruins, Cowdray Park
Midhurst, West Sussex GU29 9AL
01730 816881
www.roominthegarden.com

Elegant rusted iron arches, gazebos and pavilions.

Sitting Spiritually
Bramble Hayes, Yawl Hill Lane
Uplyme, Lyme Regis
Dorset DT7 3RP
01297 443084 | 07837 651283
www.sittingspiritually.co.uk

Martin Young is a highly respected creator of handmade swing seats and garden chairs.
Page 95, row 2, no.1

Sleeper Supplies Ltd
PO Box 1377, Kirk Sandall
Doncaster Dn3 1XT
0845 230 8866
www.sleeper-supplies.co.uk

Specialises in the supply of new and used railway sleepers, crossing timbers and telegraph poles.

Specialist Aggregates Ltd
162 Cannock Road
Stafford ST17 0QJ
01785 661018
www.specialistaggregates.com

Chippings, gravel, cobbles, pebbles, rocks and slate by 1 tonne or half tonne load.

Jonathan Stockton
Woodbridge Studios
93 Allington Road
newick, East Sussex Bn8 4nD
01825 722271
www.johnathanstockton.co.uk

Designer and maker of contemporary chic outdoor furniture. The quality of design, materials and craftsmanship mean that the pieces can be left outdoors all year and are equally suited for yachts, pools and ski chalets as well as the garden.
Page 101

Stonemarket Ltd
Oxford Road
Ryton on Dunsmore
Warwickshire CV8 3EJ
02476 518700
www.stonemarket.co.uk

Paving, walling, brick, granite, decorative aggregates (pebbles, cobbles, boulders, slate).

Sunny Aspects Ltd
36 Udney Park Road
Teddington
Middlesex TW11 9BG
0870 803 4149
info@sunnyaspects.com

Frosted translucent polypropylene fence panels for patios, windows in boundary fencing and walltops. Resistant to U.V. rays and low temperatures.

Teak and Garden BU
Ambachtstraat 10
nL-3732 Cn de Bilt
The netherlands
0031 (0) 30 220 2157
www.teak-garden.nl

Comprehensive range of garden furniture, bronze urns, tubs and statuary.

Tendercare
Southlands Road, Denham
Uxbridge, Middlesex UB9 4HD
01895 835544
www.tendercare.co.uk

A source of mature specimens of hardy plants beloved of top garden designers, has a section devoted to large scale topiary plants of all types.

Terrace and Garden Ltd
Mace's Farm, Rickling Green
nr Saffron Walden
Essex CB11 3YG
01799 543289
www.terraceandgarden.com

Garden benches for indoor, conservatory or occasional outdoor use.
Page 90, row 2, no.2

Time Circles
Seringfold, Barhatch Lane
nr Cranleigh, Surrey GU6 7nH
01483 548555
www.timecircles.co.uk

Unusual stones and sculpture, including holed stones, megaliths and symbol stones. Thirty to forty pieces on show.

The UK Gate Company
Units E17 and E18 Soulton Road
Wem Industrial Estate
Wem, Shropshire SY4 5SD
0800 783 4831 | 01939 235550
www.theukgatecompany.com

Choose from a range of existing styles or have one built from your own design from a choice of timbers or iron. With an optional automation system.

The Victorian Gate and Seating Company
Hascoll's Farm, Lower Durston
Taunton, Somerset TA3 5AH
01823 412351
www.gardenseats.com

Traditional style iron garden seats, chairs and gates. Appointment only.

Top Topiary
Cargate House, 33 Fitzroy Road
Fleet, Hampshire GU51 4JW
01252 642285
www.toptopiary.co.uk

The nursery in Crookham Village near Fleet has a wide range of high quality topiary for sale or hire at very affordable prices.

Walcot Reclamation
108 Walcot St, Bath BA1 5BG
01225 444404
www.walcot.com

Staddle stones, birdbaths, millstones, urns, troughs, sundials and pots.

Sarah Walton
Keeper's, Bo-Peep Lane
Selmeston, Nr Polegate
East Sussex Bn26 6UH
01323 811517
www.sarahwalton.co.uk

Sarah Walton produces five shapes of birdbath. All stand on green oak bases the height of which can be specified by the customer. The birdbaths are frost-proof and able to stand outdoors throughout an English winter. Also produces saltglazed tiles. Page 143

Whichford Pottery
Whichford
nr Shipton-on-Stour
Warwickshire CV36 5PG
01608 684416
www.whichfordpottery.com

Using throwing and pressing techniques passed down over centuries, the highly skilled potters at Whichford Pottery are dedicated to making only the finest terracotta flowerpots. All Whichford flowerpots carry a 10-year frost-proof guarantee and can be left outside all year round.

Wilstone
Wilstone House, Wilstone
Church Stretton
Shropshire SY6 7HW
01694 771800
www.wilstone.com

Hand-carved stone, wrought-iron and bespoke architectural pieces.
Page 70, row 2, no.3
Page 71, row 3, no.3 & 4
Page 71, row 4, no.1
Page 100, top left
Page 106, bottom right
Page 108, top centre
Page 112, top left
Page 116, row 5, no.2
Page 151, row 3, no.2

D.W. Windsor
Pindar Road, Hoddesdon
Hertfordshire En11 0DX
01992 474600
www.dwwindsor.co.uk

Over 30 designs of contemporary style seats and benches.

Woodlodge Products Ltd
Woodlodge, Holloway Hill
Chertsey KT16 0AE
01932 579100
www.woodlodge.co.uk

Major distributor of plant containers from the Far East to UK garden centres.

Acknowledgements

Well, did you count them?

How could you? I have no clue as to precisely how many ideas there are here – most of the pictures have a multitude in each. They are the work of many thousands of gardeners, builders, craftsmen and householders over many years. Thanks to their enthusiasm, care and attention, passion and ingenuity we can be encouraged to try a bit harder in our search for a more original solution, so that we, too, can inspire others. My thanks to all those who have opened their gardens to my eclectic eye – and to all of us. That's the thing about gardeners: their generosity. Most great gardens, wherever they are, are full of ideas just waiting to be enjoyed, adopted and reapplied. In fact, you might say that's what gardening is all about – putting your own interpretation on the standard formula. Except that nothing is standard. Just looking around, you can see that things are being reinvented all the time – new products, new concepts, new technology. Garden designers are some of the most creative people, and their task is, perhaps, the most difficult, because they're dealing with elements that are so unpredictable and with ingredients (plants) that never stay the same from one week to the next, one year to the next. Perhaps that's why gardening is so exciting, so frustrating, so rewarding.

My sincere thanks to all those who have helped with this book in other ways, too. Neighbours, friends and family whose gardens I've included or who have taken me to see some amazing gardens over the years: Suzanne Slesin, Sherri Donghia, Terence Conran, Stan Lovenworth, Sam Tallerico, Norman Camm, Drew Cliff, Darren Rees, Brian Thompson, Hardy Jones, Susan Scrymgour and Gladys Cliff. Thanks, too, to the manufacturers and craftsmen who sent me pictures of their products. In particular: Lee Galea, Richard Player, Andrew Crace, Jonathan Stockton, John McMillan, Sarah Walton, Chris Lewis, Chris Nangle, Martin Young and Rosemary Case.

In Britain, The National Gardens Scheme is a tremendous organisation that allows us to see hundreds of small private gardens. By contrast, the National Trust plays an important role in restoring, promoting and maintaining gardens all over the country, and the Royal Horticultural Society is the UK's leading gardening charity, dedicated to advancing horticulture and promoting good gardening through their annual and monthly shows and their own gardens at Wisley, Rosemoor, Harlow Carr, and Hyde Hall. For more information, log on to www.rhs.org.uk.

For their enthusiastic hands-on help in the production of this book I must thank the devoted commitment of Jane O'Shea, Katherine Case, Samantha Rolfe and Laura Herring, the production team at Quadrille, led by Vincent Smith and Bridget Fish, and the continued help and support of John Scott.

Page 4 © Corinne Korda/Redcover.com
Pages 6–7 © Andrew Lawson
Page 8 © Fritz von der Schulenburg – The Interior Archive/designer: John Stefanidis
Page 11 © Andrew Lawson/designer: Christopher Bradley-Hole, RHS Chelsea 2005
Page 87 Garden Picture Library/Mark Bolton
Page 97 Andrew Lawson/The Garden Collection
Page 115 Frieder Blickle/Bilderberg
Page 119 Liz Eddison/The Garden Collection: Prieuré Notre-Dame d'Orsan, France
Pages 124–5 © Elizabeth Whiting & Associates/Alamy
Page 129 © Jerry Harpur/design: Ursel Gut for The Schneider Garden
Page 134 GAP Photos/John Glover, Row 3, No.2
Page 133 © Andrew Lawson/Private Garden, Quebec
Page 161 GAP Photos/Mark Bolton, The Abbey House Gardens
Page 165 © Ed Wheeler/CORBIS, Gardens of Quinta da Bacalhoa, Portugal
Page 174 Nicola Stocken Tomkins/The Garden Collection: Wayford Manor

Editorial Director Jane O'Shea
Art Director Helen Lewis
Designer/Photographer Stafford Cliff
Picture Research Samantha Rolfe
Design Assistant Katherine Case
Editor Laura Herring
Production Vincent Smith, Bridget Fish

First published in 2007 by
Quadrille Publishing Limited
Alhambra House
27–31 Charing Cross Road
London WC2H 0LS
www.quadrille.co.uk

Design and layout © 2007
Quadrille Publishing Limited
Text © 2007 Stafford Cliff